Thank you for the purchase of this practice exam. Hopefully you'll find it to contribute to your success in passing the CIPP/E exam. The questions of this practice exam have been phrased to come as close as possible to the type and difficulty of questions you will face on the CIPP/E exam, including a number of scenario questions.

The content of this practice exam is based on the latest exam blueprint to make sure that all domains are covered to the correct extent. In addition, the questions of the different domains have been mixed to disrupt the flow and train your brain to switch between domains.

There are no instructions on how to take this practice exam, because whether you use pen and paper or write in this document (hopefully not on your e-reader) is completely up to you. However, flagging questions can be extremely useful. Train yourself in marking a question you don't immediately know the answer. This allows you to get back to the question later (if you have time left), and you will greatly increase your chances of passing the exam.

There are 90 questions, for which you can take 2,5 hours. The available information regarding the percentage of questions you'll need to answer correctly is vague, but if you score about 80% you should be ready.

The first part of this document contains the practice exam, followed by the answer key. The second part contains the same questions, with the correct answer marked and some more information to lead you to the correct answer, as well as to show you how you could have been tricked into choosing the incorrect answer.

Good luck!

1. There can be several parties involved in data processing. Which of the following is most likely true for the different parties involved?
A. The controller can be held responsible for processing without a legal basis
B. The processor can be held responsible for the instructions followed
C. The data controller is responsible for third-party behavior after fulfilling a legal obligation
D. The Data Protection Authority enforces data processing agreements

2. In case a high-impact data breach has occurred, which of the following is most likely accurate?
A. The breach needs to be reported within 72 hours after noticing it
B. An organization needs to wait until sufficient information is available about the breach
C. The data subjects need to be informed right after discovering the breach
D. In lieu of a Data Protection Officer, the Chief Information Security Officer is in charge of determining whether a breach needs to be reported to the Data Protection Authority

3. After receiving a data access request from a data subject, which of the following is most likely the case?
A. The Data Protection Officer is in charge of coordinating the data access request
B. Data access requests are preferably submitted in digital form
C. All e-mails about the data subject need to be provided during an access request
D. An organization does not have to provide access within two months

4. If an organization in the US chooses not to become Privacy Shield certified (assuming Privacy Shield is still valid), what is most likely the case?
A. The organization opted to use model clauses instead
B. The organization is not in compliance with Privacy Shield requirements
C. The organization is of limited size and excluded from international data transfer
D. Binding Corporate Rules are audited more frequently than Privacy Shield requirements

5. In case a data processor discovers a data breach, which of the following is likely not true?
A. The Data Processor is required to report violations to the controller
B. Responsibility for cooperation is part of the Data Processing Agreement
C. If the data breach is significant, the processor is required to inform the data subjects
D. The breach needs to be reported to the Data Controller without undue delay

6. Amongst the following, which best fits the description of Binding Corporate Rules?
A. An excerpt and reconciliation of applicable international data protection legislation
B. The organizational chart and intercontinental attribution of data protection responsibilities composed by the global Data Protection Officer
C. A fleshed-out version of standard contractual clauses, with only the critical parts signed
D. A legally binding document applicable to every member of a group's undertaking

7. Which of the following is the most appropriate definition of a data subject?
A. A photograph
B. An amount of research data
C. An identifiable person whose data will be deleted
D. A European corporation collecting data on non-European citizens

8. Regarding sub-processors, which of the following statements is most appropriate?
A. Only intercontinental sub-processing requires an article 32 agreement
B. A Data Processing Agreement does not necessarily apply to sub-processors
C. Sub-processors are automatically bound by a Data Processing Agreement, even if they are contracted after the original Data Processing Agreement
D. A special clause needs to be part of the Data Processing Agreement, regarding the auditing of sub-processors

9. A parcel delivery service has scanning devices equipped with GPS trackers and management can see where the vehicles are at all times. Which of the following is likely true?
A. The tracking of company property needs to be proportional and necessary
B. If the GPS signals are not needed, Privacy by Design would be to turn them off
C. In case the drivers don't take lunch breaks at home, nothing personal is revealed, and the location data is not personal data
D. Consent is the only possible valid lawful processing criterion from article 6 of the GDPR

10. By which treaty was the European Economic Community established?
A. The treaty of Paris
B. The treaty of Maastricht
C. The treaty of Rome
D. The treaty of Lisbon

11. There is more than one source of data protection legislation. Which ones provide the biggest protection in Europe?
A. The Children Online Privacy Protection Act and the Protection of Personal Information Act
B. The General Data Protection Regulation and the e-Privacy directive
C. The European Convention of Human Rights and the Data Retention Directive
D. Binding Corporate Rules and Standard Contractual Clauses

12. Which of the following is the only, or most relevant, EU legislation applicable to marketing via e-mail?
A. The General Data Protection Regulation
B. The Children Online Privacy Protection Act
C. The e-Privacy directive
D. The Controlling the Assault of Non-Solicited Pornography And Marketing Act

13. Which of the following most likely does not fall within the scope of the GDPR?
A. Public data about politicians
B. Anything about a random person
C. Information manifestly made public about unmasked IP addresses
D. Data which is subject to automated processing, such as decision making

14. When is what was previously considered personal data, not considered personal data anymore (choose the most complete answer)?
A. At the moment no location data is present
B. At times where the identifiers are scrambled
C. When the data has been manifestly made public
D. When it cannot be traced back to a natural person

15. Which of the following entities most likely qualifies for being offered a Data Processing Agreement?
A. A sporting goods store with a large customer database
B. A mail delivery service keeping a list of home addresses at the request of a corporate customer
C. A storage service that stores data for individuals
D. A data broker, illegally having collected data

16. When would the GDPR likely apply to a Canadian company?
A. When Croatian currency can be used for purchases
B. When the .ca website attracts European customers, selling medication and storing sensitive personal data
C. At the moment PIPEDA is applicable
D. If the website is visited by a large number of European citizens

17. Which of the following most likely falls within the scope of the GDPR?
A. An Austrian individual mining for photos on social media for his private database
B. An Italian church posting information on a memorial service with the name of the deceased member
C. An individual's family photos being printed
D. A Greek company selling lists of all corporations in the area

18. An organization sells food products from Europe by mail, which of the following is likely applicable?
A. The GDPR does not apply if customers order for personal use
B. When only food products are sold, no personal data is processed
C. If an order is placed, this constitutes consent
D. Handling personal data digitally is unavoidable, and handling data is processing

19. When a company in the US targets European citizens, what is likely the case?
A. The e-Privacy directive is not applicable outside of Europe, and there is no regulation of direct marketing
B. Data security safeguards are primarily required and administration security cannot clash
C. When targeting European citizens, the GDPR applies
D. US marketing requires approval of the US privacy ombudsman

20. Which of the following can be considered an example of the principle of storage limitation?
A. When a data subject is requesting access and access is denied
B. Before deleting data, making sure it was accurate when used
C. If regular audits are performed for the right amount of data being collected
D. At the moment personal data becomes outdated or is no longer needed, it is deleted

21. Which of the following can best be seen as an example of the purpose limitation principle?
A. Access is only provided after a background check
B. When the data encryption fits the level of protection required
C. When the data is deleted after the purpose has been achieved
D. The Chief Information Security Officer determines the level of protection

22. Confidentiality is important. Which of the following treats personal data with the required level of confidentiality?
A. Higher levels of security measures are in place for data collected from individuals
B. The privacy notice is clear about the level of protection provided
C. Information is only shared with the persons that need to have access to the required information for use towards the purpose for which it was collected
D. When the information is provided before collecting personal data from the data subjects

23. Accuracy is a principle best shown in which of the following?
A. Making sure no unauthorized deletion of the personal data takes place
B. Data subjects are able to update their data
C. A high level of encryption is used to prevent alteration of the personal data
D. Personal data is collected from data subjects directly rather than through third parties

24. In which of the following situations is consent most likely not required?
A. If public sensitive personal data is involved in some way
B. A survey with a reward at the end does not require consent
C. If other lawful processing criteria do not apply
D. When the interests of the controller don't outweigh those of the data subject or other parties

25. The lawful processing criterion "performance of a contract" is most likely applicable in which of the following?
A. A CCTV camera to guard inventory in a convenience store
B. Data processed to invite employees to a corporate event
C. Posting photos on social media of paying visitors to an event you organized
D. The processing of the CV of a job applicant

26. Which of the following most likely constitutes a legal obligation as meant in article 6c of the GDPR?
A. Identification numbers recorded by government institutions
B. A leaflet sent on request of the data subject for a legally required event
C. Posting images on social media without objection
D. A doctor asking legally required consent for the processing of medical data

27. When you are an employer, and one of your employees is in the hospital and the hospital urgently needs information from you regarding the activities of your employee, which of the following is most likely applicable?
A. Performance of a contract, as you have the employee under contract
B. Task carried out in the public interest, as this is in the public interest
C. Consent (sensitive personal data), as this is up to the employee
D. Vital interest, as the information could add to the treatment

28. Transparency in the context of data protection, is best described by which of the following?
A. Providing a privacy notice explaining what is done with the collected data, by whom and why
B. Asking for consent in a specific way after collecting personal data from a data subject
C. Requiring consent as a condition for using a service
D. Informing data subjects of their rights of erasure after collecting their data

This case should be used for the following four questions:

A language school teaches partly online. Students can sign up and learn a new language by clicking images and completing phrases. The results are fed back to the individual by e-mail and stored on a cloud-based server.

Students of the regular offline classroom training are also entitled to the online classes, as it is included in their study fee. On the first day of class, the students are asked to consent to the processing of their data or they are unable to use the online version of the language training.

One day, one of the students tries to access his study results and is accidentally able to see the results of his fellow students, including other details about them. This is due to a temporary security issue with the server. The student mentions the occurrence to the online trainer, who mentions it to the cloud-based server company and the problem is solved within minutes.

The language training company has over 5000 paying members, 4500 of which are taking classes online only and use a username that doesn't necessarily reflect their actual name. Account numbers with which the payments are made are the only thing that can always be traced back to an individual.

29. Which of the following is likely true regarding the incident where the data of others was accessible to one of the students?
A. As there are only usernames and results visible, this does not constitute personal data and this should not be regarded as a data breach
B. An analysis should be made as to what exactly happened in order to determine the course of action
C. Given the amount of data leaked, the breach has to be reported within 72 hours
D. The Data Protection Officer has the legal responsibility to report the data breach to the Data Protection Authority

30. Which of the following is likely true about the consent provided for the processing of data for the online classes?
A. Consent was not specific, as it was provided only after payment of the classes
B. Consent was not required, as the processing is part of the contract
C. Given that usernames are not necessarily personal data, consent is not required
D. The nature of the processing, as well as the sensitivity of the data, does not require consent

31. What is an example of a layered privacy notice on the website of the language training company?
A. A privacy notice on each sub-section of the training website, so that the notice is always visible and accessible
B. A notice with reference to the overall privacy policy, in case users want to deepen their understanding of the company's privacy practices
C. A notice where a section can be unfolded for every area of interest, such as for only the portion and the classroom training

D. A notice that contains all the contact details, for the Chief Privacy Officer as well as any Data Protection Officers under its management

32. The privacy notice for the online and classroom training needs to contain all elements that the GDPR requires in a readable way. Which of the following is not a required element?
A. The contact person at the Data Protection Agency
B. Contact details of the Data Protection Officer
C. A mention of who the controller is
D. A description of third parties involved

33. What cannot be said about fair processing notices?
A. The GDPR contains more requirements than the Data Protection Directive
B. If possible, a fair processing notice needs to be provided before collecting personal data
C. Part of a fair processing notice is the third party who ordered the data collection
D. Methods to provide fair processing notices were specified in the Data Protection Directive

34. If a company is ordered to collect data from data subjects by another company, which of the following is likely the case?
A. The contact details of the third party don't have to be disclosed, because they are not directly involved
B. The controller for which the data is collected needs to be identified
C. Due to determining how the data is collected, the third party has become the processor and the party the data collected for is a separate controller
D. The signed data processing agreement needs to be made available to the data subjects upon request

35. If you are monitoring the visitors of your website to analyze the referrer of your visitors, by recording which website the visitor visited before, which of the following is most appropriate?
A. Visitors come to the website voluntarily, and are generally aware of this type of tracking being used and have chosen to either adapt their browser settings or not
B. Masking the IP address
C. The fair processing notice afterward is sufficient, as article 14 of the GDPR allows for a fair processing notice to be delivered after if there is no other option
D. The referring website will need to incorporate in their fair processing notice that links lead to registration of their visit

36. If an organization refuses a request to delete a data subject's data, what could be the case?
A. No Data Protection Officer has been appointed, which counts as a valid reason for delaying the response to an access request or deletion request
B. The data subject refuses to drop by to show his/her ID due to travel restrictions
C. Financial regulations require to have the data
D. The data subject has provided consent prior to May 25th, 2018

37. Which of the following is likely the case in a data portability request?

A. The personal data has to be provided in machine-readable format

B. The controller has the right to prevent a data subject from providing the personal data to another controller

C. The right to data portability includes non-personal data, as the data subject provided the data

D. A data subject wishing to make use of his right to data portability is obliged to provide a safe means of transferring the data, e.g. an encrypted USB drive

This case should be used for the following three questions:

A real estate company that mostly sells apartments, started renting out a small number of apartments. It is not its core business, but more a way to make the most money out of the type of apartment that won't sell for a high price, yet is located perfectly for those that are not planning to live in the apartment for longer than three years.

The company processes small amounts of personal data, far from on a large scale. Because of that, it has not paid much attention to the GDPR and its consequences. When the hype was at its peak, right before May 25th, 2018, the company followed the 10 steps the Data Protection Authority posted on its website. The company reckons that it is compliant, especially given its data processing inventory and privacy notice on the website.

Then, a tenant informs the company that he is canceling the lease. This happens all the time, and as the area is in high demand the company puts out an advertisement expecting to quickly find a new tenant. The tenant is legally obliged to cooperate with showing the apartment to potential new tenants, so to make this process more efficient the company lists the name and phone number of the current tenant under the advertisement for making an appointment to look at the apartment.

38. What can be said about the legal obligation to cooperate with showing the apartment to potential new tenants?
A. This warrants the posting of the phone number, as this is the reasonably required means of communication
B. There are other ways of contacting the current tenant, hence no processing of personal data is allowed
C. The legal obligation can likely not be performed without the processing of personal data
D. Only the phone number was allowed to be placed on the advertisement, not the name of the current tenant

39. If the year is 2020, what can be said about when the listing of the phone number in the advertisement was mentioned in the fair processing notice?
A. As the practice was known before, and the tenant did not object, listing the information is fine
B. As the processing is required for a legal obligation, there is no need to list the processing in the fair processing notice
C. Because the tenant lived in the apartment from before May 25th, 2018, there is no reason to ask for consent for the mentioning of the phone number
D. The fair processing notice means nothing in this context as the data processing is excessive

40. If it turns out the phone number and name were not allowed to be published, which of the following would most likely be the case?
A. There is a case of unlawful processing
B. Publishing the phone number is considered a data breach
C. Publishing the name is considered a data breach
D. The current tenant is able to force the real estate agency to take down all printed adds

41. When processing personal data, appropriate technical and organizational measures are required. Which of the following is the most appropriate example of such measures?
A. Security measures adjusted to the level of risk, periodically re-evaluated
B. Automatically updated top of the line security
C. A Chief Information Security Officer has written a security policy
D. A requirement for full encryption and access through a single person

42. If an external contractor is used for handling employees' salary payments, which of the following is most likely the case?
A. Binding Corporate Rules need to be in place and approved by the Data Protection Authority
B. Approval from the Data Protection Authority for the Data Protection Impact Assessment
C. If the contractor was engaged before May 25th, 2018, no additional actions are required
D. A Data Processing Agreement is required

43. After an organization has discovered a data breach, which of the following is the most appropriate response?
A. Filing a claim against any processor after being found responsible for the breach
B. Calling the Data Protection Authority to request their expertise to aid the investigation
C. Attempting to find out what has been breached exactly
D. Informing all your data subjects regarding the breach immediately after finding out about the breach

44. In case a processor reports a data breach to the controller, which of the following is most likely the case?
A. The main one to take action is the processor, as the processor is the responsible party
B. The data breach needs to be recorded and potentially reported to the Data Protection Authority
C. No action is required if approved Binding Corporate Rules are in place
D. No action is required if a Data Processing Agreement is in place

45. Which of the following likely does not require a Data Protection Agreement?
A. A delivery service that delivers to its corporate client's employees' private address
B. A company analyzing a list of public personal data you provide it
C. A food delivery service that has been asked to deliver three gluten-free meals because there are employees with a gluten allergy
D. The cloud server where your company's files are stored

46. In case of a data breach, which of the following would most likely require communication to the data subjects?
A. The publishing of a large list of IP-addresses
B. A laptop with heavy encryption and a data self-destruct mechanism (kill-switch) has been lost, and there is only one back-up
C. An e-mail was wrongfully addressed, revealing sensitive data about someone
D. A doctor has told his family about a celebrity he has under treatment

47. As security is important, which of the following is most accurate?
A. The ability to prove processing with the appropriate level of security is present for both the processor and the controller
B. The responsibility for security can be outsourced by contracting a processor
C. Different security standards apply to a data processor and a controller
D. The processor has no duty in taking action when red flags arise

48. Which of the following likely does not constitute a data breach?
A. A folder left open to public access
B. Damaging a hard drive with secure encryption without having a backup
C. A laptop stolen, but password protected
D. Processing personal data without the required data processing agreement

49. Privacy by Design (and default) is a set of principles to incorporate in the design process. Which of the following is not a good example of Privacy by Design?
A. Information is only collected after it is required
B. Having the option to configure the browser to automatically reject tracking cookies
C. Cookie requests are automatically rejected, even functional cookies
D. The connection to the internet is kept to a minimum

50. Which of the following would most likely require a Data Protection Impact Assessment?
A. When processing the data of an indigenous tribe for research that falls under a scientific exception and no consent needs to be obtained
B. Re-performing high-risk processing, where vulnerable children are interviewed on a large scale and the data is stored for a long time
C. Replacing the CCTV cameras used for a university building
D. When working with incredibly sensitive personal data, after being rendered irreversibly anonymous

51. How can a Data Protection Impact Assessment best be described?
A. An assessment of the impact of the processing operations on the protection of personal data
B. An analysis for the best level of protection at the most reasonable cost
C. A document in the context of data protection that is a required part of a data inventory
D. The Data Protection Officer is required to sign off on the Data Protection Impact Assessment

52. A Data Protection Officer is not always mandatory. In which of the following is it not mandatory to appoint one?
A. For a court acting in its judicial capacity
B. For a public authority processing very little personal data
C. If a company engages often in regular and systematic monitoring of data subjects on a large scale
D. If the core activities of the organization consist of processing on a large scale of special categories of personal data

53. Of the actions that can be required of a Data Protection Officer, which of the following cannot be required?
A. Decide on the course of action of the organization, balancing all costs and benefits
B. Inform the organization of its data protection obligations
C. Hold his finger at the pulse of the organization and monitor GDPR compliance
D. Write the report of a data breach to support reporting a breach to the Data Protection Authority

54. Which of the following best fits the description of (the now possibly defunct) Privacy Shield?
A. A collection of policies and procedures approved by the Data Protection Authority, where the organization's data exchange has taken place
B. Contracts, approved by the US ombudsman and audited before becoming certified
C. It is an inter-company agreement, with at least one of the affiliates based in the United States, with approval of the designated Data Protection Authority
D. A framework for transatlantic exchanges of personal data for commercial purposes

55. On September 2020, which of the following countries did not have a positive adequacy decision?
A. New Zealand
B. Australia
C. Jersey
D. Guernsey

56. Which of the following is most likely to enforce/execute the legislation of the European Union by means of implementing and monitoring compliance?
A. The European Court of Auditors
B. The European Parliament
C. The European Council
D. The European Commission

57. When would you most likely use model clauses for international data transfers?
A. When an international data transfer takes place to a governmental organization for processing in a country that is only partially adequate
B. Supplementary to the processor being Privacy Shield (or its replacement) certified
C. Despite Binding Corporate Rules being in place, if a country is not on the adequacy list
D. The amount of anonymized sensitive data reaches over 100.000 data elements

58. All of the following are true, except for which?
A. Standard contractual clauses can be freely adjusted to fit the specifics of the exchange
B. Each legal entity has to sign the Binding Corporate Rules
C. There is no need for standard contractual clauses if an adequacy decision is in place
D. If the Data Protection Authority approves Binding Corporate Rules, transfers can be made to countries without an adequacy decision

59. Even if a country has an adequacy decision, which of the following is still necessary?
A. A data processing agreement, in case of processors and sub-processors
B. Binding Corporate Rules, depending on the sensitivity of the data subjects
C. Standard contractual clauses, depending on the number of parties involved
D. Alternative Transfer mechanisms, if the data subjects object

60. Of the following statements, which is most untrue regarding Binding Corporate Rules?
A. If the Binding Corporate Rules don't cover certain countries, model clauses are required
B. The Data Protection Authority is required to approve the Binding Corporate Rules
C. Binding Corporate Rules can only be approved in the country at the headquarters of the organization
D. Binding Corporate Rules are in no way, shape, or form a replacement for a Data Processing Agreement

61. The European Union's institutions are subject to frequent audits. Which European institution performs these audits most?
A. The European Court of Auditors
B. The European Parliament
C. The European Council
D. The European Central Bank

62. How is the establishment of an adequacy decision most accurately described?
A. The European Data Protection Supervisor assures the controls in place in a country to determine their adequacy
B. A political struggle where trade interests are theoretically the deciding factor
C. The European Commission assesses the country's legislation and international commitments
D. An application takes place and a decision is reached

63. Which of the following has been introduced by the GDPR?
A. Model clauses for international data transfer
B. Sub-processor contract requirements
C. Codes of conduct for international data transfer
D. Controller to controller model clauses

64. If a multinational and intercontinental organization has affiliates in several EU countries, which of the following is true?
A. Data transfers are limited to the countries where model clauses have been signed
B. The supervisory authority of the main/single establishment of the controller shall be competent to act as the lead supervisory authority
C. Multinational organizations only answer to the European Data Protection Supervisor
D. If the headquarters of the multinational in a country with an adequacy decision, no Data Protection Officer is required to be appointed

65. Privacy is a right provided in article 8 of the European Convention of Human rights. Which of the following is most applicable?
A. Privacy is an absolute right, uncompromised by others
B. Privacy is more important than the freedom of other people
C. Privacy results in restricted freedom to spread opinions
D. Privacy is not an absolute right

66. Which of the following least correctly describe the tasks of a Data Protection Authority?
A. To promote awareness and understanding of data protection
B. To handle complaints and carry out investigations
C. To provide tools and templates for GDPR implementation
D. To monitor development of ICT and commercial practices

67. Which of the following is most true about the European Data Protection Board?
A. The European Data Protection Supervisor is a collection of heads of national Data Protection Authorities
B. The European Data Protection Board supervises data protection practices at the European Commission
C. The European Data Protection Board supervises the Privacy Shield implementation for certified organizations
D. Article 29 Working Party was similar to the European Data Protection Board

68. Which of the following is most likely true regarding the European Data Protection Supervisor?
A. The opinions issued by the European Data Protection Supervisor are fully enforceable as law
B. The staff of the European Commission reports to the European Data Protection Supervisor
C. The European Data Protection Supervisor has the authority to issue revisions of the GDPR
D. The European Data Protection Supervisor, due to its authority and expertise, has the power to overturn any judicial decision

69. Regarding the fines under the GDPR, which of the following is most likely true?
A. The fine for a violation is 4% of the global annual turnover or 20 million Euros
B. The fine will be proportionate to the violation, so not necessarily 20 million Euros
C. The maximum fine is 10 Million Euros for companies operating on a national level, and 20 Million Euros for a company operating on a global level
D. The measures an organization has in place do not influence any possible fine

70. If an organization is investigated by the Data Protection Authority, which of the following will most likely not apply in the context of that investigation?
A. The Data Protection Authority has the authority to request access to the results of the organization's internal audits
B. A full search of the certifications published on the company website can be performed
C. The individuals are held accountable for a lack of cooperation
D. Access to the premises can be part of the investigation of the Data Protection Authority

71. If unlawful processing of personal data takes place, and the data controller is found guilty, which of the following is most likely true?
A. It is up to the data processor to prove he is not to blame
B. The amount claimable is 2% of the global turnover
C. Any damages can only be claimed in the national court
D. The damage can be material or non-material

72. When an employer processes personal data, which of the following is most likely not true?
A. For the sensitive personal data, consent was required
B. Data processing is allowed if the employer has a legitimate interest
C. There are legal obligations that require the employer to process the employee's personal data
D. Even before employment, the processing can be necessary for the performance of a contract

73. Which of the following statements is most likely not true regarding workplace monitoring?
A. In many cases a privacy notice is required, informing the employees in which way they are possibly monitored
B. The Data Protection Officer is required to sign off on the Data Protection Impact Assessment
C. A Data Protection Impact Assessment is required
D. The works council has influence regarding workplace monitoring

74. Regarding the use of personal electronics at work, which of the following is most appropriate?
A. If an organization wants to be responsible, it provides a budget to employees
B. A Bring Your Own Device policy should be created
C. The company should make it mandatory for the employee to back up his device to the company cloud, for which a Data Processing Agreement is in place
D. The processing that takes place on the employees' personal devices can't be part of the data inventory

This case should be used for the following three questions:

A European train company makes most of its money selling train travels, both domestically and internationally. You were just appointed to the position of Data Protection Officer, and as such have access to all information regarding the way the train company processes personal data. This is quite an exciting opportunity for you, and you want everyone in the company to like you.

Even though the train company sells a lot of tickets, the competition from cheap airlines is noticeable. The train company needs to lower the prices to become competitive. In addition, it started making money by other means, such as by selling the illusion of priority boarding and selling lottery tickets and overpriced cheap perfume and jewelry.

A new and innovative way the train company intends to make extra money is by targeted advertising. First, the free Wi-Fi on the train will track the browsing habits of travelers. This is something that is agreed to, otherwise, there won't be access to the Wi-Fi. This allows the train company to sell advertisements based on the browsing habits of the traveler. Second, for the travelers that have reserved a seat, a specific advertisement will be displayed in front of their seat based on the travel history that consists of the frequency and location.

75. After reading the handover note from the previous Data Protection Officer that just said "good luck", you get the feeling it was sarcastic. Which of the following can be said about the situation at the train company?
A. There is no need to take action, as the details are not yet clear and there could be an explanation for everything
B. It is obvious that the data collection is not in compliance for the Wi-Fi tracking, and immediate action is needed to stop the practice
C. It is obvious that the data collection is not in compliance and the travel history is misused, and immediate action is needed to stop the practice
D. It could be the case that the customer is aware of all practices and consents to all use of the data as it provides cheaper travel

76. Which of the following is most likely true regarding the consent obtained for the Wi-Fi tracking?
A. It is difficult, or even impossible, to obtain consent that is specific enough
B. If there are children on the train that can result in vulnerable data subjects from whom valid consent cannot be required
C. The train conductors also use Wi-Fi, and employee/employer consent is never valid
D. The requirement of consent is an issue in most, if not all, cases in this scenario

77. Which of the following is true regarding the use of the travel history of travelers?
A. Buying a train ticket means that you agree to the privacy notice posted on the website
B. The selling of targeted advertisement is likely forbidden, as it includes transferring personal data to third parties
C. Since the train company needs to keep up with budget airlines, the practice can easily be justified, regardless of any third-party involvement
D. It is processing for a new purpose and it is likely required to provide an opportunity to object to the processing

78. If an employer wants to install CCTV, which of the following is most likely true?
A. If the works council provides approval, the organization can install CCTV
B. Due to the employment at will, the legitimate interest balance will almost certainly be in the employer's favor
C. If CCTV is the cheapest option to solve a vandalism issue, there is sufficient legitimate interest
D. If the legitimate interest criterion is used and privacy notices are visible before entering the premises so there is no secret recording

79. In case an online shop wants to send a marketing e-mail, which of the following is most likely true?
A. A prior customer relationship and the opportunity to opt-out were needed before sending the e-mail
B. A data broker's list of contacts can be purchased, if obtained from outside of the EU
C. If publicly available information is used, no prior relationship or consent is needed
D. An e-mail sent without an applicable processing ground constitutes a data breach

80. Which of the following is most true regarding marketing e-mails versus regular mail marketing?
A. The same rules apply to both e-mail and regular mail marketing
B. Article 6 of the GDPR is not applicable to e-mail marketing, as the e-privacy directive applies
C. The e-privacy directive covers only the marketing via e-mail
D. Regular mail greatly reduces the risk of a data breach

81. If a website contains a web beacon, which of the following is likely correct?
A. A web beacon on a website is locally hosted and causes no external contact
B. Browser settings can result in the rejection of known web beacons
C. Using a web beacon, only an IP address, and whether the web beacon has been loaded, can be seen by the placer of the web beacon
D. Profiling using web beacons in combination with social media can be performed without collecting personal data

82. Regarding the processing of the personal data of children, which of the following is most appropriate?
A. Parents need to be notified in every case the personal data of their children is processed
B. Depending on the country, there could be different rules
C. The data of children is considered sensitive personal data
D. Children can fill out a declaration replacing parental consent

83. When a real estate agency re-uses a photo taken at an open house, this time for marketing purposes, which of the following is most appropriate?
A. Depending on the exposure of the marketing campaign, consent is required
B. Visitors can reasonably expect there to be photos taken and used as the real estate agency wishes
C. In case children are visible in the photo, both parents are required to provide consent
D. Consent is required regardless of any pre-contractual relationship

84. If an organization uses data from public websites, for its marketing, which of the following is most true?
A. When the data has been mined from a public source it falls outside of the scope of the GDPR
B. Depending on whether the data is mined inside or outside of the EU is of importance
C. Only information that is publicly available in the EU falls under the scope of the GDPR
D. A lawful processing criterion will need to be applicable

85. How can cloud computing best be described?
A. Any storage of data on an externally hosted server
B. The hosting of intranet pages that are not accessible to outsiders
C. The use of dynamic IP addresses to make the person less identifiable
D. Phone towers connecting individual devices and logging the activity

86. Cookies may or may not require consent. Of the following, which do most likely not require consent?
A. Functional Cookies
B. Tracking cookies
C. Web beacons
D. Analytical cookies

87. Which of the following is most likely not true regarding social networks?
A. Sensitive personal data shared on a social networking website is considered manifestly made public
B. Anything a person does while logged in can be considered personal data
C. Uploading photos of race does not require consent
D. Using social media websites is not considered implicit consent for further processing

88. Search engine operators can process personal data in some cases. Which of the following is likely true?
A. Search engine operators require consent before processing search commands
B. Search engines are always considered processors
C. Search engines fall outside of the scope of the GDPR
D. Data retention periods must be proportional to the purpose of collection

89. If a social media website uses face recognition to determine race and then labels its users accordingly, which of the following is likely true?
A. Any online appearance is manifestly made public, no consent is required for further processing
B. Consent is required for the processing of race
C. The use of facial recognition is appropriate
D. Unless the data subject objects, the practice is acceptable

90. Social media websites make use of privacy notices to inform data subjects. Which of the following is likely not true?
A. The privacy notice needs to be concise and in an easily accessible form
B. Transparency is a requirement of the privacy notice
C. The privacy notice needs to be intelligible for the target audience
D. The consequences of actions on social media are predictable and commonly known, and for that reason don't require any information to be communicated

Correct answers:

1A, 2A, 3D, 4A, 5C, 6D, 7C, 8B, 9A, 10C, 11B, 12C, 13D, 14D, 15B, 16A, 17C, 18D, 19C, 20D, 21C, 22C, 23B, 24A, 25D, 26A, 27D, 28A, 29B, 30B, 31C, 32A, 33D, 34B, 35B, 36C, 37A, 38C, 39D, 40A, 41A, 42D, 43C, 44B, 45C, 46C, 47A, 48D, 49B, 50A, 51A, 52A, 53A, 54D, 55B, 56D, 57A, 58A, 59A, 60C, 61A, 62C, 63C, 64B, 65D, 66C, 67D, 68B, 69B, 70C, 71D, 72A, 73B, 74B, 75A, 76D, 77D, 78D, 79A, 80C, 81B, 82B, 83D, 84D, 85A, 86A, 87A, 88D, 89B, 90D

1. There can be several parties involved in data processing. Which of the following is most likely true for the different parties involved?

A. The controller can be held responsible for processing without a legal basis (correct)

B. The processor can be held responsible for the instructions followed

C. The data controller is responsible for third-party behavior after fulfilling a legal obligation

D. The Data Protection Authority enforces data processing agreements

More information:

The controller is the one determining the means and purpose, and as such is responsible for anything illegal that happens under its control, which certainly is processing without a legal basis. It reads controller rather than data controller, to mislead. Don't be fooled.

2. In case a high-impact data breach has occurred, which of the following is most likely accurate?

A. The breach needs to be reported within 72 hours after noticing it (correct)

B. An organization needs to wait until sufficient information is available about the breach

C. The data subjects need to be informed right after discovering the breach

D. In lieu of a Data Protection Officer, the Chief Information Security Officer is in charge of determining whether a breach needs to be reported to the Data Protection Authority

More information:

A high-impact data breach likely needs to be reported to the Data Protection Authority, which needs to happen within 72 hours after discovering the data breach.

3. After receiving a data access request from a data subject, which of the following is most likely the case?
A. The Data Protection Officer is in charge of coordinating the data access request
B. Data access requests are preferably submitted in digital form
C. All e-mails about the data subject need to be provided during an access request
D. An organization does not have to provide access within two months (correct)
More information:
A data access request can be extended twice, with a month. So, the total time would be three months.

4. If an organization in the US chooses not to become Privacy Shield certified (assuming Privacy Shield is still valid), what is most likely the case?
A. The organization opted to use model clauses instead (correct)
B. The organization is not in compliance with Privacy Shield requirements
C. The organization is of limited size and excluded from international data transfer
D. Binding Corporate Rules are audited more frequently than Privacy Shield requirements
More information:
There is no requirement to be Privacy Shield certified. It helps but is not required. In certain cases, model clauses can be a more convenient way to comply with the requirements.
Note that Privacy Shield is not valid anymore (September 2020). However, the exam can still contain questions about it, and the mechanisms can become relevant again in the future.

5. In case a data processor discovers a data breach, which of the following is likely not true?
A. The Data Processor is required to report violations to the controller
B. Responsibility for cooperation is part of the Data Processing Agreement
C. If the data breach is significant, the processor is required to inform the data subjects (correct)
D. The breach needs to be reported to the Data Controller without undue delay
More information:
Data processors don't communicate to data subjects. The controller determines whether communication with the data subjects takes place.

6. Amongst the following, which best fits the description of Binding Corporate Rules?
A. An excerpt and reconciliation of applicable international data protection legislation
B. The organizational chart and intercontinental attribution of data protection responsibilities composed by the global Data Protection Officer
C. A fleshed-out version of standard contractual clauses, with only the critical parts signed
D. A legally binding document applicable to every member of a group's undertaking (correct)
More information:
Binding Corporate Rules are rules within a company that operates in several countries, including outside of the EU.

7. Which of the following is the most appropriate definition of a data subject?

A. A photograph

B. An amount of research data

C. An identifiable person whose data will be deleted (correct)

D. A European corporation collecting data on non-European citizens

More information:

A person about whom there is data is a data subject. If it will be deleted, means it has not yet been deleted. Keep an eye out for tricky phrasing.

8. Regarding sub-processors, which of the following statements is most appropriate?

A. Only intercontinental sub-processing requires an article 32 agreement

B. A Data Processing Agreement does not necessarily apply to sub-processors (correct)

C. Sub-processors are automatically bound by a Data Processing Agreement, even if they are contracted after the original Data Processing Agreement

D. A special clause needs to be part of the Data Processing Agreement, regarding the auditing of sub-processors

More information:

A Data Processing Agreement does not automatically apply to sub-processors. A clause needs to be included, and the processor needs a contract with the sub-processor so the appropriate level of control regarding the processing practices is established.

The Data Protection Agreement between processor and controller likely contains a clause requiring permission from the controller to use sub-processors.

9. A parcel delivery service has scanning devices equipped with GPS trackers and management can see where the vehicles are at all times. Which of the following is likely true?

A. The tracking of company property needs to be proportional and necessary (correct)

B. If the GPS signals are not needed, Privacy by Design would be to turn them off

C. In case the drivers don't take lunch breaks at home, nothing personal is revealed, and the location data is not personal data

D. Consent is the only possible valid lawful processing criterion from article 6 of the GDPR

More information:

Every processing of personal data needs to be proportional and necessary. So regardless of the example, the processing needs to be proportional and necessary. Option B may seem correct, but in the case of Privacy by Design, they would be turned off by default.

10. By which treaty was the European Economic Community established?

A. The treaty of Paris

B. The treaty of Maastricht

C. The treaty of Rome (correct)

D. The treaty of Lisbon

More information:

You should be able to find this fact in your textbook. If you got this wrong, it is advisable to reread the information or your summary of the information.

11. There is more than one source of data protection legislation. Which ones provide the biggest protection in Europe?
A. The Children Online Privacy Protection Act and the Protection of Personal Information Act
B. The General Data Protection Regulation and the e-Privacy directive (correct)
C. The European Convention of Human Rights and the Data Retention Directive
D. Binding Corporate Rules and Standard Contractual Clauses
More information:
The GDPR and the e-Privacy directive both apply in the EU and are more specific than the other regulation mentioned. Binding Corporate Rules and Standard Contractual Clauses only provide protection for the personal data processed by the organizations bound by them.

12. Which of the following is the only, or most relevant, EU legislation applicable to marketing via e-mail?
A. The General Data Protection Regulation
B. The Children Online Privacy Protection Act
C. The e-Privacy directive (correct)
D. The Controlling the Assault of Non-Solicited Pornography And Marketing Act
More information:
The e-Privacy directive contains specific requirements for electronic communication. The GDPR also provides protection, but the e-Privacy directive has further requirements.

13. Which of the following most likely does not fall within the scope of the GDPR?
A. Public data about politicians
B. Anything about a random person
C. Information manifestly made public about unmasked IP addresses
D. Data which is subject to automated processing, such as decision making (correct)
More information:
Data used in automated processing falls outside of the scope of the GDPR unless it is personal data. Read questions carefully, so you won't be tricked. The answer reads data, which does not necessarily include personal data, so if the other options are true this one is the one to consider false due to its incompleteness. Regard unmasked IP addresses as personal data, especially since a web beacon with social media combination where social media websites use web beacons to find out which IP address belongs to which person at which time.

14. When is what was previously considered personal data, not considered personal data anymore (choose the most complete answer)?
A. At the moment no location data is present
B. At times where the identifiers are scrambled
C. When the data has been manifestly made public
D. When it cannot be traced back to a natural person (correct)
More information:
When something cannot be traced back to a natural person, it is not personal data. This has to be irreversible.

15. Which of the following entities most likely qualifies for being offered a Data Processing Agreement?
A. A sporting goods store with a large customer database
B. A mail delivery service keeping a list of home addresses at the request of a corporate customer (correct)
C. A storage service that stores data for individuals
D. A data broker, illegally having collected data
More information:
When personal data is processed by one organization (the processor) at the request of another organization (the controller), there is a controller and a processor. Hence, a data processing agreement is required. A list of home addresses is personal data, and when kept at the request of another organization a data processing agreement is likely required.

16. When would the GDPR likely apply to a Canadian company?
A. When Croatian currency can be used for purchases (correct)
B. When the .ca website attracts European customers, selling medication and storing sensitive personal data
C. At the moment PIPEDA is applicable
D. If the website is visited by a large number of European citizens
More information:
If a non-EU website targets EU citizens, the GDPR likely applies. Using the currency of a country from the EU (Croatia) can be seen as targeting citizens from that country (and the EU).

17. Which of the following most likely falls within the scope of the GDPR?
A. An Austrian individual mining for photos on social media for his private database
B. An Italian church posting information on a memorial service with the name of the deceased member
C. An individual's family photos being printed (correct)
D. A Greek company selling lists of all corporations in the area
More information:
Photos with people (data subjects) on them are (or contain) personal data. Deceased people fall outside of the scope of the GDPR. Personal use also falls outside of the scope of the GDPR.

18. An organization sells food products from Europe by mail, which of the following is likely applicable?
A. The GDPR does not apply if customers order for personal use
B. When only food products are sold, no personal data is processed
C. If an order is placed, this constitutes consent
D. Handling personal data digitally is unavoidable, and handling data is processing (correct)
More information:
When shipping per mail, at the very least an address needs to be known. An address in combination with order information is likely personal data.

19. When a company in the US targets European citizens, what is likely the case?
A. The e-Privacy directive is not applicable outside of Europe, and there is no regulation of direct marketing
B. Data security safeguards are primarily required and administration security cannot clash
C. When targeting European citizens, the GDPR applies (correct)
D. US marketing requires approval of the US privacy ombudsman
More information:
When EU citizens are targeted, the GDPR applies.

20. Which of the following can be considered an example of the principle of storage limitation?
A. When a data subject is requesting access and access is denied
B. Before deleting data, making sure it was accurate when used
C. If regular audits are performed for the right amount of data being collected
D. At the moment personal data becomes outdated or is no longer needed, it is deleted (correct)
More information:
Storage limitation means storing something for as short of a period as possible. As short as possible will likely practically translate to no longer than absolutely necessary.

21. Which of the following can best be seen as an example of the purpose limitation principle?
A. Access is only provided after a background check
B. When the data encryption fits the level of protection required
C. When the data is deleted after the purpose has been achieved (correct)
D. The Chief Information Security Officer determines the level of protection
More information:
Purpose limitation means limiting the processing to only that processing which is necessary for the purpose for which it was collected. Once that purpose has been achieved, there is no reason to store it any longer. Storing is also processing, hence this would likely result in processing the data beyond the purpose for which it was collected.

22. Confidentiality is important. Which of the following treats personal data with the required level of confidentiality?
A. Higher levels of security measures are in place for data collected from individuals
B. The privacy notice is clear about the level of protection provided
C. Information is only shared with the persons that need to have access to the required information for use towards the purpose for which it was collected (correct)
D. When the information is provided before collecting personal data from the data subjects
More information:
Confidentiality practically means sharing the data with as few persons as possible (only those who need the data to fulfill the purpose). This can, for example, be achieved through access restriction.

23. Accuracy is a principle best shown in which of the following?
A. Making sure no unauthorized deletion of the personal data takes place
B. Data subjects are able to update their data (correct)
C. A high level of encryption is used to prevent alteration of the personal data
D. Personal data is collected from data subjects directly rather than through third parties
More information:
Accuracy means that the personal data is accurate enough for the purpose for which it was collected. Letting users update their data themselves is likely good for keeping it accurate (unless people change it incorrectly, for fun, or mistakenly). Collecting directly from data subjects is also a good option, but this doesn't keep it accurate.

24. In which of the following situations is consent most likely not required?
A. If public sensitive personal data is involved in some way (correct)
B. A survey with a reward at the end does not require consent
C. If other lawful processing criteria do not apply
D. When the interests of the controller don't outweigh those of the data subject or other parties
More information:
When sensitive personal data has been manifestly made public, the processing restriction does not apply. This means consent is not necessarily required anymore. A valid lawful processing criterion is still required, it just doesn't necessarily have to be consent.

25. The lawful processing criterion "performance of a contract" is most likely applicable in which of the following?
A. A CCTV camera to guard inventory in a convenience store
B. Data processed to invite employees to a corporate event
C. Posting photos on social media of paying visitors to an event you organized
D. The processing of the CV of a job applicant (correct)
More information:
Even before signing an employment contract, all required processing for the recruitment process can be seen as the performance of a contract (pre-contractual phase).

26. Which of the following most likely constitutes a legal obligation as meant in article 6c of the GDPR?
A. Identification numbers recorded by government institutions (correct)
B. A leaflet sent on request of the data subject for a legally required event
C. Posting images on social media without objection
D. A doctor asking legally required consent for the processing of medical data
More information:
Government institutions are legally required to process identification numbers. Hence, it is a process for which the processing of personal data is legally required, and article 6c applies. Part of a process that works towards fulfilling a legal obligation, but isn't necessary to fulfill that legal obligation, may not necessarily rely on article 6c.

27. When you are an employer, and one of your employees is in the hospital and the hospital urgently needs information from you regarding the activities of your employee, which of the following is most likely applicable?

A. Performance of a contract, as you have the employee under contract

B. Task carried out in the public interest, as this is in the public interest

C. Consent (sensitive personal data), as this is up to the employee

D. Vital interest, as the information could add to the treatment (correct)

More information:

Likely saving someone's life by processing personal data can rely on the vital interest lawful processing criterion.

28. Transparency in the context of data protection, is best described by which of the following?

A. Providing a privacy notice explaining what is done with the collected data, by whom and why (correct)

B. Asking for consent in a specific way after collecting personal data from a data subject

C. Requiring consent as a condition for using a service

D. Informing data subjects of their rights of erasure after collecting their data

More information:

Article 13 of the GDPR lists the information that needs to be provided. This is often referred to as a privacy notice.

This case should be used for the following four questions:

A language school teaches partly online. Students can sign up and learn a new language by clicking images and completing phrases. The results are fed back to the individual by e-mail and stored on a cloud-based server.

Students of the regular offline classroom training are also entitled to the online classes, as it is included in their study fee. On the first day of class, the students are asked to consent to the processing of their data or they are unable to use the online version of the language training.

One day, one of the students tries to access his study results and is accidentally able to see the results of his fellow students, including other details about them. This is due to a temporary security issue with the server. The student mentions the occurrence to the online trainer, who mentions it to the cloud-based server company and the problem is solved within minutes.

The language training company has over 5000 paying members, 4500 of which are taking classes online only and use a username that doesn't necessarily reflect their actual name. Account numbers with which the payments are made are the only thing that can always be traced back to an individual.

29. Which of the following is likely true regarding the incident where the data of others was accessible to one of the students?
A. As there are only usernames and results visible, this does not constitute personal data and this should not be regarded as a data breach
B. An analysis should be made as to what exactly happened in order to determine the course of action (correct)
C. Given the amount of data leaked, the breach has to be reported within 72 hours
D. The Data Protection Officer has the legal responsibility to report the data breach to the Data Protection Authority
More information:
Before concluding whether something is a data breach and determining whether action needs to be taken, more information is needed. There are deadlines (72 hours), but before the deadline, it is advisable to collect sufficient information (as far as possible).

30. Which of the following is likely true about the consent provided for the processing of data for the online classes?
A. Consent was not specific, as it was provided only after payment of the classes
B. Consent was not required, as the processing is part of the contract (correct)
C. Given that usernames are not necessarily personal data, consent is not required
D. The nature of the processing, as well as the sensitivity of the data, does not require consent
More information:
If something is necessary for the performance of a contract, there already is a lawful processing criterion. You can still ask for consent, but it is not needed (and not advisable).

31. What is an example of a layered privacy notice on the website of the language training company?

A. A privacy notice on each sub-section of the training website, so that the notice is always visible and accessible

B. A notice with reference to the overall privacy policy, in case users want to deepen their understanding of the company's privacy practices

C. A notice where a section can be unfolded for every area of interest, such as for only the portion and the classroom training (correct)

D. A notice that contains all the contact details, for the Chief Privacy Officer as well as any Data Protection Officers under its management

More information:

Layered privacy notices consist of different layers. Each layer goes deeper, so for every area the revealing of a layer should show more information. So, option C is correct. Option B could also be correct, but information is missing. Be wary of this during the exam, and choose the most complete correct answer.

32. The privacy notice for the online and classroom training needs to contain all elements that the GDPR requires in a readable way. Which of the following is not a required element?

A. The contact person at the Data Protection Agency (correct)

B. Contact details of the Data Protection Officer

C. A mention of who the controller is

D. A description of third parties involved

More information:

The contact person at the Data Protection Agency does not need to be mentioned. Also, it is Authority and not Agency. There is no specific contact person (likely), hence this would practically be impossible too. See article 13 of the GDPR for more information regarding what needs to be provided.

33. What cannot be said about fair processing notices?
A. The GDPR contains more requirements than the Data Protection Directive
B. If possible, a fair processing notice needs to be provided before collecting personal data
C. Part of a fair processing notice is the third party who ordered the data collection
D. Methods to provide fair processing notices were specified in the Data Protection Directive (correct)
More information:
The Data Protection Directive did not specify methods of providing a fair processing notice.

34. If a company is ordered to collect data from data subjects by another company, which of the following is likely the case?
A. The contact details of the third party don't have to be disclosed, because they are not directly involved
B. The controller for which the data is collected needs to be identified (correct)
C. Due to determining how the data is collected, the third party has become the processor and the party the data collected for is a separate controller
D. The signed data processing agreement needs to be made available to the data subjects upon request
More information:
The controller always needs to be made known. For more information see article 14 of the GDPR.

35. If you are monitoring the visitors of your website to analyze the referrer of your visitors, by recording which website the visitor visited before, which of the following is most appropriate?

A. Visitors come to the website voluntarily, and are generally aware of this type of tracking being used and have chosen to either adapt their browser settings or not

B. Masking the IP address (correct)

C. The fair processing notice afterward is sufficient, as article 14 of the GDPR allows for a fair processing notice to be delivered after if there is no other option

D. The referring website will need to incorporate in their fair processing notice that links lead to registration of their visit

More information:

Unmasked IP addresses can possibly be considered personal data. Masking them results in making it more difficult to trace back to an individual.

36. If an organization refuses a request to delete a data subject's data, what could be the case?

A. No Data Protection Officer has been appointed, which counts as a valid reason for delaying the response to an access request or deletion request

B. The data subject refuses to drop by to show his/her ID due to travel restrictions

C. Financial regulations require to have the data (correct)

D. The data subject has provided consent prior to May 25th, 2018

More information:

There are financial regulations that require the keeping of certain financial data, for example as documents to be shown during a tax audit. If this contains personal data, then this likely does not have to be deleted during an access request. Option D may also be correct, but is less likely and physically dropping by with an ID is not the only way a data subject can identify himself.

37. Which of the following is likely the case in a data portability request?

A. The personal data has to be provided in machine-readable format (correct)

B. The controller has the right to prevent a data subject from providing the personal data to another controller

C. The right to data portability includes non-personal data, as the data subject provided the data

D. A data subject wishing to make use of his right to data portability is obliged to provide a safe means of transferring the data, e.g. an encrypted USB drive

More information:

To comply with a data portability request, the personal data has to be provided in machine-readable form. The other options contain false statements.

This case should be used for the following three questions:

A real estate company that mostly sells apartments, started renting out a small number of apartments. It is not its core business, but more a way to make the most money out of the type of apartment that won't sell for a high price, yet is located perfectly for those that are not planning to live in the apartment for longer than three years.

The company processes small amounts of personal data, far from on a large scale. Because of that, it has not paid much attention to the GDPR and its consequences. When the hype was at its peak, right before May 25th, 2018, the company followed the 10 steps the Data Protection Authority posted on its website. The company reckons that it is compliant, especially given its data processing inventory and privacy notice on the website.

Then, a tenant informs the company that he is canceling the lease. This happens all the time, and as the area is in high demand the company puts out an advertisement expecting to quickly find a new tenant. The tenant is legally obliged to cooperate with showing the apartment to potential new tenants, so to make this process more efficient the company lists the name and phone number of the current tenant under the advertisement for making an appointment to look at the apartment.

38. What can be said about the legal obligation to cooperate with showing the apartment to potential new tenants?
A. This warrants the posting of the phone number, as this is the reasonably required means of communication
B. There are other ways of contacting the current tenant, hence no processing of personal data is allowed
C. The legal obligation can likely not be performed without the processing of personal data (correct)
D. Only the phone number was allowed to be placed on the advertisement, not the name of the current tenant
More information:
There is no need to process the personal data in the way that it was processed. The company could have sent a message to the tenant and have not published the phone number. For example, the company could have physically visited the tenant and asked for a spare key so they could show the apartment to the potential new tenants. There will, however, likely always be processing of personal data, but the invasiveness of publishing a private phone number is somewhat excessive.

39. If the year is 2020, what can be said about when the listing of the phone number in the advertisement was mentioned in the fair processing notice?

A. As the practice was known before, and the tenant did not object, listing the information is fine

B. As the processing is required for a legal obligation, there is no need to list the processing in the fair processing notice

C. Because the tenant lived in the apartment from before May 25th, 2018, there is no reason to ask for consent for the mentioning of the phone number

D. The fair processing notice means nothing in this context as the data processing is excessive (correct)

More information:

Illegitimate processing is not made legitimate by placing it in a fair processing notice, especially since the fair processing notice was likely not provided a few years ago when the personal data was collected from the tenant.

40. If it turns out the phone number and name were not allowed to be published, which of the following would most likely be the case?

A. There is a case of unlawful processing (correct)

B. Publishing the phone number is considered a data breach

C. Publishing the name is considered a data breach

D. The current tenant is able to force the real estate agency to take down all printed adds

More information:

When you process when it is not allowed, that is unlawful processing.

41. When processing personal data, appropriate technical and organizational measures are required. Which of the following is the most appropriate example of such measures?

A. Security measures adjusted to the level of risk, periodically re-evaluated (correct)

B. Automatically updated top of the line security

C. A Chief Information Security Officer has written a security policy

D. A requirement for full encryption and access through a single person

More information:

Appropriate technical and organizational measures are adjusted to the level of risk and the current technological possibilities. Hence, periodically there should be re-evaluation to see whether the measures are still appropriate.

42. If an external contractor is used for handling employees' salary payments, which of the following is most likely the case?

A. Binding Corporate Rules need to be in place and approved by the Data Protection Authority

B. Approval from the Data Protection Authority for the Data Protection Impact Assessment

C. If the contractor was engaged before May 25th, 2018, no additional actions are required

D. A Data Processing Agreement is required (correct)

More information:

Employee salary information is personal data and an external contractor can be considered a processor, hence a Data Processing Agreement is required.

43. After an organization has discovered a data breach, which of the following is the most appropriate response?
A. Filing a claim against any processor after being found responsible for the breach
B. Calling the Data Protection Authority to request their expertise to aid the investigation
C. Attempting to find out what has been breached exactly (correct)
D. Informing all your data subjects regarding the breach immediately after finding out about the breach
More information:
After a data breach, it is of utmost importance to find out what exactly happened. This is to confirm whether personal data has indeed been leaked, how the problem can be solved, what actions need to be taken to protect the data subjects, etc.

44. In case a processor reports a data breach to the controller, which of the following is most likely the case?
A. The main one to take action is the processor, as the processor is the responsible party
B. The data breach needs to be recorded and potentially reported to the Data Protection Authority (correct)
C. No action is required if approved Binding Corporate Rules are in place
D. No action is required if a Data Processing Agreement is in place
More information:
Depending on the size and effects of the breach, action needs to be taken by the controller. The processor follows the controller's instructions, hence the controller generally determines what the course of action is.

45. Which of the following likely does not require a Data Protection Agreement?

A. A delivery service that delivers to its corporate client's employees' private address

B. A company analyzing a list of public personal data you provide it

C. A food delivery service that has been asked to deliver three gluten-free meals because there are employees with a gluten allergy (correct)

D. The cloud server where your company's files are stored

More information:

The delivery of gluten-free meals is not processing of personal data, unless the gluten-free meals are reserved for specific persons (and their names are mentioned somewhere) and that is somehow captured or communicated rather than a company ordering three gluten-free meals just in case there are people with a gluten allergy.

46. In case of a data breach, which of the following would most likely require communication to the data subjects?
A. The publishing of a large list of IP-addresses
B. A laptop with heavy encryption and a data self-destruct mechanism (kill-switch) has been lost, and there is only one back-up
C. An e-mail was wrongfully addressed, revealing sensitive data about someone (correct)
D. A doctor has told his family about a celebrity he has under treatment
More information:
A wrongly addressed e-mail is considered a data breach (and one that is quite common), and when it reveals sensitive data it likely has consequences for the data subjects and therefore requires to be communicated to them so they can take action if needed. It reads sensitive data and not sensitive personal data, to mislead.

47. As security is important, which of the following is most accurate?
A. The ability to prove processing with the appropriate level of security is present for both the processor and the controller (correct)
B. The responsibility for security can be outsourced by contracting a processor
C. Different security standards apply to a data processor and a controller
D. The processor has no duty in taking action when red flags arise
More information:
Both the processor and the controller are required to operate with the appropriate level of security. The controller is responsible, as long as the processor follows the controller's instructions.

48. Which of the following likely does not constitute a data breach?
A. A folder left open to public access
B. Damaging a hard drive with secure encryption without having a backup
C. A laptop stolen, but password protected
D. Processing personal data without the required data processing agreement (correct)
More information:
If there is no data processing agreement, that does not necessarily mean there was a data breach. It does mean that the organizational security measures are not appropriate.

49. Privacy by Design (and default) is a set of principles to incorporate in the design process. Which of the following is not a good example of Privacy by Design?
A. Information is only collected after it is required
B. Having the option to configure the browser to automatically reject tracking cookies (correct)
C. Cookie requests are automatically rejected, even functional cookies
D. The connection to the internet is kept to a minimum
More information:
The mere option to configure the browser this way is not optimal. Having it enabled by default would be more Privacy by Design.

50. Which of the following would most likely require a Data Protection Impact Assessment?

A. When processing the data of an indigenous tribe for research that falls under a scientific exception and no consent needs to be obtained (correct)

B. Re-performing high-risk processing, where vulnerable children are interviewed on a large scale and the data is stored for a long time

C. Replacing the CCTV cameras used for a university building

D. When working with incredibly sensitive personal data, after being rendered irreversibly anonymous

More information:

If data processing falls under the scientific exemption, this does not mean no security measures have to be taken. These security measures can be based on the outcome of a Data Protection Impact Assessment.

51. How can a Data Protection Impact Assessment best be described?

A. An assessment of the impact of the processing operations on the protection of personal data (correct)

B. An analysis for the best level of protection at the most reasonable cost

C. A document in the context of data protection that is a required part of a data inventory

D. The Data Protection Officer is required to sign off on the Data Protection Impact Assessment

More information:

A Data Protection Impact Assessment is basically a risk assessment. So, it concerns looking at the risk and how to reduce the risk to an acceptable level.

52. A Data Protection Officer is not always mandatory. In which of the following is it not mandatory to appoint one?
A. For a court acting in its judicial capacity (correct)
B. For a public authority processing very little personal data
C. If a company engages often in regular and systematic monitoring of data subjects on a large scale
D. If the core activities of the organization consist of processing on a large scale of special categories of personal data
More information:
Courts acting in their judicial capacity don't need a Data Protection Officer. See article 37 of the GDPR.

53. Of the actions that can be required of a Data Protection Officer, which of the following cannot be required?
A. Decide on the course of action of the organization, balancing all costs and benefits (correct)
B. Inform the organization of its data protection obligations
C. Hold his finger at the pulse of the organization and monitor GDPR compliance
D. Write the report of a data breach to support reporting a breach to the Data Protection Authority
More information:
A Data Protection Officer needs to be independent. If he assumes responsibility and has to balance all aspects (meaning decide on what to do, not just whether something is compliant), independence is highly likely impaired.

54. Which of the following best fits the description of (the now possibly defunct) Privacy Shield?
A. A collection of policies and procedures approved by the Data Protection Authority, where the organization's data exchange has taken place
B. Contracts, approved by the US ombudsman and audited before becoming certified
C. It is an inter-company agreement, with at least one of the affiliates based in the United States, with approval of the designated Data Protection Authority
D. A framework for transatlantic exchanges of personal data for commercial purposes (correct)
More information:
Privacy Shield is (or used to be) a framework for transatlantic exchanges of data for commercial purposes. The US has been left out in the answer, but it is still the most correct answer. Don't forget that these kinds of tricks will be applied to mislead you during the exam.

55. On September 2020, which of the following countries did not have a positive adequacy decision?
A. New Zealand
B. Australia (correct)
C. Jersey
D. Guernsey
More information:
In September 2020, Australia had no positive adequacy decision.

56. Which of the following is most likely to enforce/execute the legislation of the European Union by means of implementing and monitoring compliance?
A. The European Court of Auditors
B. The European Parliament
C. The European Council
D. The European Commission (correct)
More information:
The European Commission is the one enforcing/executing legislation. This is quite basic knowledge, so if you didn't answer this correctly it is recommendable to reread the chapter on the European Union. There will be several questions about the European Union, its functioning, and its origin on the exam (however irrelevant for GDPR implementation).

57. When would you most likely use model clauses for international data transfers?
A. When an international data transfer takes place to a governmental organization for processing in a country that is only partially adequate (correct)
B. Supplementary to the processor being Privacy Shield (or its replacement) certified
C. Despite Binding Corporate Rules being in place, if a country is not on the adequacy list
D. The amount of anonymized sensitive data reaches over 100.000 data elements
More information:
Canada is a partially adequate country. Its government did not receive an adequate decision, so extra measures are required.

58. All of the following are true, except for which?

A. Standard contractual clauses can be freely adjusted to fit the specifics of the exchange (correct)

B. Each legal entity has to sign the Binding Corporate Rules

C. There is no need for standard contractual clauses if an adequacy decision is in place

D. If the Data Protection Authority approves Binding Corporate Rules, transfers can be made to countries without an adequacy decision

More information:

Standard contractual clauses are not allowed to be freely adjusted.

59. Even if a country has an adequacy decision, which of the following is still necessary?

A. A data processing agreement, in case of processors and sub-processors (correct)

B. Binding Corporate Rules, depending on the sensitivity of the data subjects

C. Standard contractual clauses, depending on the number of parties involved

D. Alternative Transfer mechanisms, if the data subjects object

More information:

An adequacy decision does not remove the need for a data processing agreement.

60. Of the following statements, which is most untrue regarding Binding Corporate Rules?
A. If the Binding Corporate Rules don't cover certain countries, model clauses are required
B. The Data Protection Authority is required to approve the Binding Corporate Rules
C. Binding Corporate Rules can only be approved in the country at the headquarters of the organization (correct)
D. Binding Corporate Rules are in no way, shape, or form a replacement for a Data Processing Agreement
More information:
If the organization has its headquarters outside of the EU, the Binding Corporate Rules cannot be approved there. So, option C is not necessarily true, and therefore most untrue of the available options.

61. The European Union's institutions are subject to frequent audits. Which European institution performs these audits most?
A. The European Court of Auditors (correct)
B. The European Parliament
C. The European Council
D. The European Central Bank
More information:
The European Court of Auditors is the external auditor of the European Union, and is mostly (only) occupied with performing audits.

62. How is the establishment of an adequacy decision most accurately described?
A. The European Data Protection Supervisor assures the controls in place in a country to determine their adequacy
B. A political struggle where trade interests are theoretically the deciding factor
C. The European Commission assesses the country's legislation and international commitments (correct)
D. An application takes place and a decision is reached
More information:
To come to an adequacy decision, the European Commission assesses the country's legislation and international commitments.

63. Which of the following has been introduced by the GDPR?
A. Model clauses for international data transfer
B. Sub-processor contract requirements
C. Codes of conduct for international data transfer (correct)
D. Controller to controller model clauses
More information:
Codes of conduct for international data transfer (Binding Corporate Rules) are new in the GDPR.

64. If a multinational and intercontinental organization has affiliates in several EU countries, which of the following is true?
A. Data transfers are limited to the countries where model clauses have been signed
B. The supervisory authority of the main/single establishment of the controller shall be competent to act as the lead supervisory authority (correct)
C. Multinational organizations only answer to the European Data Protection Supervisor
D. If the headquarters of the multinational in a country with an adequacy decision, no Data Protection Officer is required to be appointed
More information:
The main establishment in the EU is important, and the one-stop-shop for a non-EU organization.

65. Privacy is a right provided in article 8 of the European Convention of Human rights. Which of the following is most applicable?
A. Privacy is an absolute right, uncompromised by others
B. Privacy is more important than the freedom of other people
C. Privacy results in restricted freedom to spread opinions
D. Privacy is not an absolute right (correct)
More information:
Privacy is not an absolute right, there is always a balance of interests of different actors (people, institutions, etc.).

66. Which of the following least correctly describe the tasks of a Data Protection Authority?
A. To promote awareness and understanding of data protection
B. To handle complaints and carry out investigations
C. To provide tools and templates for GDPR implementation (correct)
D. To monitor development of ICT and commercial practices
More information:
A Data Protection Authority is not required to provide tools and templates for GDPR implementation. Organizations are responsible for creating/purchasing their own tools and templates (except perhaps for communicating with the Data Protection Authority, such as in the case of a data breach).

67. Which of the following is most true about the European Data Protection Board?
A. The European Data Protection Supervisor is a collection of heads of national Data Protection Authorities
B. The European Data Protection Board supervises data protection practices at the European Commission
C. The European Data Protection Board supervises the Privacy Shield implementation for certified organizations
D. Article 29 Working Party was similar to the European Data Protection Board (correct)
More information:
The European Data Protection Board used to be called the Article 29 Working Party. Questions like this will be on the exam, so keep details like this in mind. Also, notice the mixing up of the terms Board and Supervisor.

68. Which of the following is most likely true regarding the European Data Protection Supervisor?
A. The opinions issued by the European Data Protection Supervisor are fully enforceable as law
B. The staff of the European Commission reports to the European Data Protection Supervisor (correct)
C. The European Data Protection Supervisor has the authority to issue revisions of the GDPR
D. The European Data Protection Supervisor, due to its authority and expertise, has the power to overturn any judicial decision
More information:
The European Data Protection Supervisor supervises the data protection practices at the European Commission.

69. Regarding the fines under the GDPR, which of the following is most likely true?
A. The fine for a violation is 4% of the global annual turnover or 20 million Euros
B. The fine will be proportionate to the violation, so not necessarily 20 million Euros (correct)
C. The maximum fine is 10 Million Euros for companies operating on a national level, and 20 Million Euros for a company operating on a global level
D. The measures an organization has in place do not influence any possible fine
More information:
Fines are proportionate. The 4% and 20 million Euros are the maximum fines, not automatically the fine that an organization will receive.

70. If an organization is investigated by the Data Protection Authority, which of the following will most likely not apply in the context of that investigation?
A. The Data Protection Authority has the authority to request access to the results of the organization's internal audits
B. A full search of the certifications published on the company website can be performed
C. The individuals are held accountable for a lack of cooperation (correct)
D. Access to the premises can be part of the investigation of the Data Protection Authority
More information:
Individuals are not held liable for a lack of cooperation. The organization is held accountable.

71. If unlawful processing of personal data takes place, and the data controller is found guilty, which of the following is most likely true?
A. It is up to the data processor to prove he is not to blame
B. The amount claimable is 2% of the global turnover
C. Any damages can only be claimed in the national court
D. The damage can be material or non-material (correct)
More information:
Material and non-material damage fall under the damages referred to in article 82 of the GDPR.

72. When an employer processes personal data, which of the following is most likely not true?
A. For the sensitive personal data, consent was required (correct)
B. Data processing is allowed if the employer has a legitimate interest
C. There are legal obligations that require the employer to process the employee's personal data
D. Even before employment, the processing can be necessary for the performance of a contract
More information:
An employer does not necessarily need consent if sensitive personal data is processed for obligations/rights in the field of employment.

73. Which of the following statements is most likely not true regarding workplace monitoring?
A. In many cases a privacy notice is required, informing the employees in which way they are possibly monitored
B. The Data Protection Officer is required to sign off on the Data Protection Impact Assessment (correct)
C. A Data Protection Impact Assessment is required
D. The works council has influence regarding workplace monitoring
More information:
A Data Protection Officer is legally required to be given the opportunity to provide his input, but it is not required to sign off on a Data Protection Impact Assessment.

74. Regarding the use of personal electronics at work, which of the following is most appropriate?

A. If an organization wants to be responsible, it provides a budget to employees

B. A Bring Your Own Device policy should be created (correct)

C. The company should make it mandatory for the employee to back up his device to the company cloud, for which a Data Processing Agreement is in place

D. The processing that takes place on the employees' personal devices can't be part of the data inventory

More information:

A Bring Your Own Device policy is an appropriate way to get the organizational measures in place for using personal electronics at work. There will likely need to be technical measures in place as well.

This case should be used for the following three questions:

A European train company makes most of its money selling train travels, both domestically and internationally. You were just appointed to the position of Data Protection Officer, and as such have access to all information regarding the way the train company processes personal data. This is quite an exciting opportunity for you, and you want everyone in the company to like you.

Even though the train company sells a lot of tickets, the competition from cheap airlines is noticeable. The train company needs to lower the prices to become competitive. In addition, it started making money by other means, such as by selling the illusion of priority boarding and selling lottery tickets and overpriced cheap perfume and jewelry.

A new and innovative way the train company intends to make extra money is by targeted advertising. First, the free Wi-Fi on the train will track the browsing habits of travelers. This is something that is agreed to, otherwise, there won't be access to the Wi-Fi. This allows the train company to sell advertisements based on the browsing habits of the traveler. Second, for the travelers that have reserved a seat, a specific advertisement will be displayed in front of their seat based on the travel history that consists of the frequency and location.

75. After reading the handover note from the previous Data Protection Officer that just said "good luck", you get the feeling it was sarcastic. Which of the following can be said about the situation at the train company?

A. There is no need to take action, as the details are not yet clear and there could be an explanation for everything (correct)

B. It is obvious that the data collection is not in compliance for the Wi-Fi tracking, and immediate action is needed to stop the practice

C. It is obvious that the data collection is not in compliance and the travel history is misused, and immediate action is needed to stop the practice

D. It could be the case that the customer is aware of all practices and consents to all use of the data as it provides cheaper travel

More information:

There is not enough information known to the Data Protection Officer yet to take action.

76. Which of the following is most likely true regarding the consent obtained for the Wi-Fi tracking?
A. It is difficult, or even impossible, to obtain consent that is specific enough
B. If there are children on the train that can result in vulnerable data subjects from whom valid consent cannot be required
C. The train conductors also use Wi-Fi, and employee/employer consent is never valid
D. The requirement of consent is an issue in most, if not all, cases in this scenario (correct)
More information:
If consent for the tracking is required in order to use the Wi-Fi, then the consent is likely not freely given. However, it first needs to be established whether there is any other applicable lawful processing criterion, such as legitimate interest.

77. Which of the following is true regarding the use of the travel history of travelers?
A. Buying a train ticket means that you agree to the privacy notice posted on the website
B. The selling of targeted advertisement is likely forbidden, as it includes transferring personal data to third parties
C. Since the train company needs to keep up with budget airlines, the practice can easily be justified, regardless of any third-party involvement
D. It is processing for a new purpose and it is likely required to provide an opportunity to object to the processing (correct)
More information:
In this instance, the lawful processing criterion is likely "legitimate interest", for which the opportunity to object needs to be in place.

78. If an employer wants to install CCTV, which of the following is most likely true?

A. If the works council provides approval, the organization can install CCTV

B. Due to the employment at will, the legitimate interest balance will almost certainly be in the employer's favor

C. If CCTV is the cheapest option to solve a vandalism issue, there is sufficient legitimate interest

D. If the legitimate interest criterion is used and privacy notices are visible before entering the premises so there is no secret recording (correct)

More information:

CCTV is most likely installed based on legitimate interests, which can be reasoned because the other lawful processing criteria likely don't apply (unless there is a legal obligation to use CCTV). It is in the employer's interest to monitor the premises to prevent theft. The data subjects need to be informed of the CCTV cameras, which needs to be done before data subjects enter the premises.

79. In case an online shop wants to send a marketing e-mail, which of the following is most likely true?

A. A prior customer relationship and the opportunity to opt-out were needed before sending the e-mail (correct)

B. A data broker's list of contacts can be purchased, if obtained from outside of the EU

C. If publicly available information is used, no prior relationship or consent is needed

D. An e-mail sent without an applicable processing ground constitutes a data breach

More information:

A prior customer relationship is required. And at the time of collecting the data, the opportunity for opting-out needs to be provided.

80. Which of the following is most true regarding marketing e-mails versus regular mail marketing?

A. The same rules apply to both e-mail and regular mail marketing

B. Article 6 of the GDPR is not applicable to e-mail marketing, as the e-privacy directive applies

C. The e-privacy directive covers only the marketing via e-mail (correct)

D. Regular mail greatly reduces the risk of a data breach

More information:

The e-privacy directive covers electronic communication, so the non-electronic-mail is not covered.

81. If a website contains a web beacon, which of the following is likely correct?
A. A web beacon on a website is locally hosted and causes no external contact
B. Browser settings can result in the rejection of known web beacons (correct)
C. Using a web beacon, only an IP address, and whether the web beacon has been loaded, can be seen by the placer of the web beacon
D. Profiling using web beacons in combination with social media can be performed without collecting personal data
More information:
A browser (for example the DuckDuckGo browser) can be programmed to reject known web beacons. It has a list of known web beacons and prevents them from being loaded.

82. Regarding the processing of the personal data of children, which of the following is most appropriate?
A. Parents need to be notified in every case the personal data of their children is processed
B. Depending on the country, there could be different rules (correct)
C. The data of children is considered sensitive personal data
D. Children can fill out a declaration replacing parental consent
More information:
Member states can choose the age limit, so it can differ per member state.

83. When a real estate agency re-uses a photo taken at an open house, this time for marketing purposes, which of the following is most appropriate?
A. Depending on the exposure of the marketing campaign, consent is required
B. Visitors can reasonably expect there to be photos taken and used as the real estate agency wishes
C. In case children are visible in the photo, both parents are required to provide consent
D. Consent is required regardless of any pre-contractual relationship (correct)
More information:
If consent is required, whether a pre-contractual relationship exists doesn't change this.

84. If an organization uses data from public websites, for its marketing, which of the following is most true?
A. When the data has been mined from a public source it falls outside of the scope of the GDPR
B. Depending on whether the data is mined inside or outside of the EU is of importance
C. Only information that is publicly available in the EU falls under the scope of the GDPR
D. A lawful processing criterion will need to be applicable (correct)
More information:
Even for personal data from public sources, a lawful processing criterion is required.

85. How can cloud computing best be described?

A. Any storage of data on an externally hosted server (correct)

B. The hosting of intranet pages that are not accessible to outsiders

C. The use of dynamic IP addresses to make the person less identifiable

D. Phone towers connecting individual devices and logging the activity

More information:

Storage of data on an externally hosted service can be considered as cloud computing.

86. Cookies may or may not require consent. Of the following, which do most likely not require consent?

A. Functional Cookies (correct)

B. Tracking cookies

C. Web beacons

D. Analytical cookies

More information:

Functional cookies are required to make a website function and don't require consent.

87. Which of the following is most likely not true regarding social networks?

A. Sensitive personal data shared on a social networking website is considered manifestly made public (correct)

B. Anything a person does while logged in can be considered personal data

C. Uploading photos of race does not require consent

D. Using social media websites is not considered implicit consent for further processing

More information:

If someone publishes something for the world to see, this can be seen as manifestly made public. However, sharing on a social network is not necessarily public (think of private messaging).

88. Search engine operators can process personal data in some cases. Which of the following is likely true?

A. Search engine operators require consent before processing search commands

B. Search engines are always considered processors

C. Search engines fall outside of the scope of the GDPR

D. Data retention periods must be proportional to the purpose of collection (correct)

More information:

There should be a reason to keep the data for as long as it is being kept.

89. If a social media website uses face recognition to determine race and then labels its users accordingly, which of the following is likely true?
A. Any online appearance is manifestly made public, no consent is required for further processing
B. Consent is required for the processing of race (correct)
C. The use of facial recognition is appropriate
D. Unless the data subject objects, the practice is acceptable
More information:
There appears to be no lawful processing criterion applicable, except for consent. For any question regarding the requirement of consent, always go over the other lawful processing criteria and assess whether they could apply or not.

90. Social media websites make use of privacy notices to inform data subjects. Which of the following is likely not true?
A. The privacy notice needs to be concise and in an easily accessible form
B. Transparency is a requirement of the privacy notice
C. The privacy notice needs to be intelligible for the target audience
D. The consequences of actions on social media are predictable and commonly known, and for that reason don't require any information to be communicated (correct)
More information:
Of course, social media websites are required to provide information about their data protection practices, regardless of how obvious the information is.